Make It Take It Crafts

Old Testament Heroes

These pages may be copied.
Permission is granted to the buyer of this book to reproduce, duplicate or photocopy student materials in this book for use with pupils in Sunday school or Bible teaching classes.

Rainbow Books

Make It Take It Crafts

Enelle Eder

Old Testament Heroes

Because of his love for the Old Testament stories, I dedicate this book to Dennis, my husband, my soulmate, my encourager, my protector and my best friend. Thanks, Honey, for making all my dreams come true!

MAKE IT • TAKE IT CRAFTS/OLD TESTAMENT HEROES
©2001 by Rainbow Publishers, second printing
ISBN 1-58411-006-6
Rainbow reorder# RB38022

Rainbow Books
P.O. Box 261129
San Diego, CA 92196

Illustrator: Chuck Galey

Scriptures are from the *Holy Bible: New International Version* (North American Edition), ©1973, 1978, 1984 by the International Bible Society. Used by permission of Zondervan Bible Publishers.

All rights reserved.

Printed in the United States of America

Table of Contents

Make It • Take It • Make It • Take It • Make It • Take It • Make It • Take It

Make It • Take It
Memory Verses

To Families

We have some exciting crafts planned for use in teaching Bible lessons. We would like to ask your help in saving or collecting the following checked items.

- ❏ bird seed
- ❏ chenille wires
- ❏ clear plastic transparencies
- ❏ clear, self-stick plastic
- ❏ clothespins
- ❏ coffee grounds
- ❏ construction paper
- ❏ cotton
- ❏ craft glue
- ❏ craft sticks
- ❏ elastic
- ❏ felt
- ❏ foam rubber
- ❏ foam trays
- ❏ frozen whipped topping lids
- ❏ gift wrap
- ❏ glitter
- ❏ gold foil

- ❏ grass seed
- ❏ greeting cards
- ❏ imitation pearls
- ❏ individual milk cartons
- ❏ ink pads
- ❏ jar lids
- ❏ jingle bells
- ❏ lace
- ❏ magnets
- ❏ packing chips
- ❏ paper fasteners
- ❏ paper plates
- ❏ paper towel tubes
- ❏ plastic canvas
- ❏ plastic communion cups
- ❏ plastic cups
- ❏ plastic drinking straws
- ❏ poster board

- ❏ potato
- ❏ potting soil
- ❏ ribbon
- ❏ sequins
- ❏ small wooden blocks
- ❏ soda top tabs
- ❏ sponge
- ❏ stickers
- ❏ tempera paint
- ❏ thread
- ❏ tissue paper
- ❏ toilet tissue rolls
- ❏ tuna cans
- ❏ wooden beads
- ❏ yarn
- ❏ yarn needles

Please bring in the items on _____

Thank you for your help!

To Families

We have some exciting crafts planned for use in teaching Bible lessons. We would like to ask your help in saving or collecting the following checked items.

- ❏ bird seed
- ❏ chenille wires
- ❏ clear plastic transparencies
- ❏ clear, self-stick plastic
- ❏ clothespins
- ❏ coffee grounds
- ❏ construction paper
- ❏ cotton
- ❏ craft glue
- ❏ craft sticks
- ❏ elastic
- ❏ felt
- ❏ foam rubber
- ❏ foam trays
- ❏ frozen whipped topping lids
- ❏ gift wrap
- ❏ glitter
- ❏ gold foil

- ❏ grass seed
- ❏ greeting cards
- ❏ imitation pearls
- ❏ individual milk cartons
- ❏ ink pads
- ❏ jar lids
- ❏ jingle bells
- ❏ lace
- ❏ magnets
- ❏ packing chips
- ❏ paper fasteners
- ❏ paper plates
- ❏ paper towel tubes
- ❏ plastic canvas
- ❏ plastic communion cups
- ❏ plastic cups
- ❏ plastic drinking straws
- ❏ poster board

- ❏ potato
- ❏ potting soil
- ❏ ribbon
- ❏ sequins
- ❏ small wooden blocks
- ❏ soda top tabs
- ❏ sponge
- ❏ stickers
- ❏ tempera paint
- ❏ thread
- ❏ tissue paper
- ❏ toilet tissue rolls
- ❏ tuna cans
- ❏ wooden beads
- ❏ yarn
- ❏ yarn needles

Please bring in the items on _____

Thank you for your help!

Introduction

All children love crafts! However, in today's fast-paced world, a simple coloring project is no longer adequate to hold a child's attention. *Make It•Take It Crafts* is a set of five books that gives you new ideas for teaching important eternal truths. These activities are designed to help you teach your children about God through Bible-based lessons.

Each of the five books contains over 25 different topics to discuss, and unique crafts to accompany them. A memory verse, which relates directly to the topic, is provided for each lesson. Encourage the children to write the memory verse on the craft whenever possible as a take-home reminder.

Detailed instructions and full-size, reproducible patterns are included for each craft. They can be made from household materials or basic craft supplies. A list of supplies is provided on page 9 in a reproducible note format so you can ask for families' assistance in collecting materials.

Each lesson is labeled according to the age appropriateness based on the subject matter and difficulty of the craft. However, use your own judgment as to which lessons and crafts are suitable for the skills and interests of your students. You will find that the lessons can be successfully adapted for use in Sunday school, children's church, vacation Bible school, Christian school or wherever God's Word is taught.

With *Make It•Take It Crafts* your children will not only make and take crafts — they will make new commitments that will take them into a life of serving the Lord.

Abraham

Ages 8-11

Memory Verse

I will surely bless you and make your descendants as numerous as the stars in the sky.

~Genesis 22:17

· ·

Reliable Abraham

Do you know what it means to be reliable? It means others can depend on you. God had a reliable servant in the Old Testament named Abraham. When God gave him a command, he carried it out. When God gave him a promise, Abraham believed that promise even when it didn't seem possible.

God had promised to make Abraham the "Father of Nations," but when he was 99 years old Abraham still did not have a son from his wife Sarah. God once again reassured Abraham that He would give them a son. Soon afterward, Isaac was born.

Sometime later God decided to test Abraham's faith. He told him to take his son Isaac up on a mountain and sacrifice him as a burnt offering. Abraham loved his son very much, but early the next morning he started to do exactly as God had told him. When he had the altar built and was just about to put Isaac on it, God stopped him. He said, "Now that I know you are willing to hold back nothing from Me, I will bless you with many offspring. Your descendants will be as many as the stars in the sky."

God knew that Abraham was reliable. He could depend on him to be obedient. Can God depend on you to be obedient, too? Be reliable like Abraham!

For Discussion

1. What does it mean to be reliable?

2. What did God promise Abraham?

3. How did God test Abraham?

Traveler's Tent

What You Need

- Abraham pattern from page 15
- felt
- craft glue
- crayons
- markers
- tape
- chenille wires
- poster board
- scissors

Before Class

Duplicate the Abraham pattern from page 15 for each child. Cut the felt into 8" x 10" pieces, one per child. Cut the chenille wire into two 10" and one 8" length per child.

What to Do

1. Show how to glue the chenille wire to the felt in an H shape as shown on the diagram. Allow the glue to dry before bending the felt into a tent shape.

2. Have the students color Abraham with crayons or markers.

3. Instruct them to glue the picture to thin poster board before cutting it out.

4. Have them write the memory verse on the back of the figure.

5. Instruct the students to cut a strip of poster board about $1/2$" x 6". Show how to fold it into a triangle loop.

6. Show where to glue one flat side of the loop to Abraham's back so he can sit up next to his tent.

Make It • Take It • Make It • Take It • Make It • Take It • Make It • Take It

Boaz

Ages 5-8

Memory Verse

Whoever is kind to the needy honors God.

~Proverbs 14:31

· ·

Merciful Boaz

Boaz was a very wealthy man. He had many animals, lots of fields full of crops and numerous servants. He lived in Bethlehem.

As Boaz checked on his harvesters one day, he noticed a beautiful young woman picking up fallen grain around the edge of his field. He asked one of his servants who she was and they explained that she and her mother-in-law had moved back from Moab. Boaz realized she was Ruth, the one who had married his distant cousin who had died. Boaz was impressed with the hard-working girl.

Boaz wanted to show mercy to Ruth, so he made special arrangements to have her glean grain only from his fields so she would be safe. He asked the harvesters to leave extra grain in the fields so that she would have a large, full basket each evening.

Then Boaz went a step further. He became the "kinsman-redeemer" for Ruth. That means he bought the property that once belonged to her father-in-law and husband. It gave him the right to claim Ruth for his wife and take care of her the rest of her life. Boaz showed mercy to Ruth out of love.

We, too, need to show mercy to others because of our love for God.

For Discussion

1. How do we know Boaz was rich?

2. How did he show mercy to Ruth?

3. How can we show mercy to others?

Thumb Body Book Mark

What You Need

- book mark from page 18
- colored poster board
- ink pad
- wet cloth
- clear, self-stick plastic
- markers
- scissors

Before Class

Duplicate the book mark from page 18 for each child onto colored poster board.

What to Do

1. Allow the students to cut out and outline the book mark in a coordinating color.

2. Write or have the students write the memory verse toward the top of the book mark.

3. Show how to use an ink pad to make three or more thumb prints on the book mark. Provide a wet cloth to wash inky fingers!

4. Have the children draw eyes, mouths, legs and arms on the thumb prints.

5. Help the students cover the book mark with clear, self-stick plastic on both sides, then cut off the extra plastic.

6. Encourage the children to give the book mark to "thumbody special"!

Make It • Take It • Make It • Take It • Make It • Take It • Make It • Take It

David

Ages 5-8

Memory Verse

Praise the Lord with the harp; make music to him.

~Psalm 33:2

David, a Man of Praise

When David was a small boy watching his father's sheep, he loved to play songs on the instruments he made and sing praises to his heavenly Father. Sitting alone on the hillside with a flock of sheep gave David lots of time to practice his music. He wrote many songs as he sat there.

Saul was the king when David was young. He was a moody person. He often became very sad and demanded that someone play music to cheer him up. When David played the harp for Saul he did it so well that Saul made him his personal attendant. Even though Saul became violent at times and David had to flee for his life, deep down Saul loved David because of his music.

The book of Psalms in the Bible is a collection of songs, prayers and praises written by David. He expressed his feelings through the psalms. We are instructed many times in the Bible to praise the Lord. Some people sing, some clap their hands and others play instruments. It isn't important what method we use as long as we remember to praise God.

For Discussion

1. What was David's job as a boy and how did he pass time?

2. Why did Saul love David?

3. Name some ways we can praise the Lord.

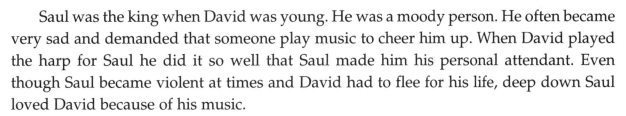

Make It • Take It • Make It • Take It • Make It • Take It • Make It • Take It

Harmonious Harp

What You Need

- harp pattern from page 21
- white poster board
- string or heavy thread
- glitter
- hole punch
- scissors
- tape
- glue
- markers

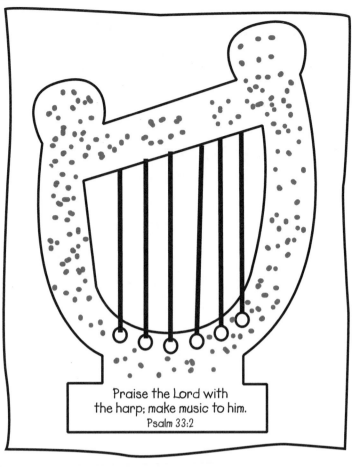

Praise the Lord with the harp; make music to him.
Psalm 33:2

Before Class

Use the pattern to cut one harp from poster board for each child. Cut the string into one 30" length per child.

What to Do

1. Show how to punch six holes across the bottom of the harp as indicated on the pattern.

2. Have the students tape one end of the string to the top back of the harp and thread it through the first hole. They should go back up to the top, tape the string and return to the next hole. Continue until the harp has been strung.

3. Instruct the children to write the memory verse at the bottom of the harp with a marker.

4. Have the students spread a thin layer of glue on the sides and top of the harp and sprinkle it with glitter.

Make It • Take It • Make It • Take It • Make It • Take It • Make It • Take It

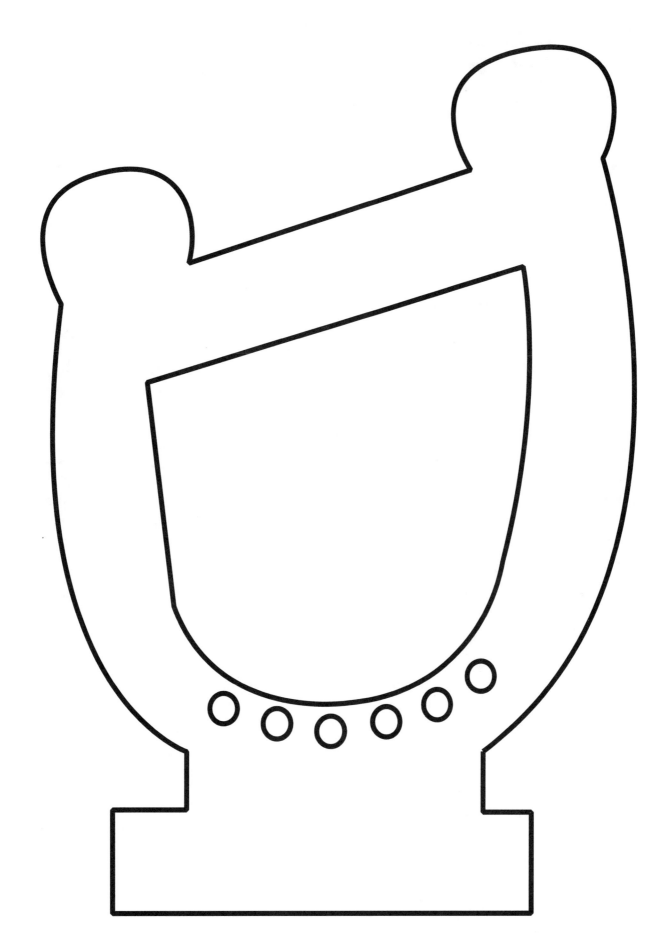

Deborah

Ages 8-11

Memory Verse

For the Lord will hand Sisera over to a woman.

~Judges 4:9

. . . .

Powerful Deborah

Deborah started out as a humble housewife whose job was lighting the lamps in the tabernacle. But because she was faithful in the small things, God gave her greater things to do.

Deborah sat under a palm tree and gave advice or counsel to the people who came to her. She became well known for her counseling and soon was recognized as a judge. She held an important position of power, especially for a woman in Bible times.

Deborah recognized that the men of Israel lacked leadership because they were afraid of their enemies. She knew that God would rescue her people if they would honor Him, so she went to a man named Barok. He was one of Israel's most capable military men. Together they made a plan of action against their enemy, Sisera.

Even though the Israelites did not have the equipment and chariots that their enemy had, they saw the confidence that Deborah had in God and went to battle. Just as they were about to start, God sent a violent sleet and hail storm directly into the faces of Sisera and his men. The heavy chariots sank deep into the mud from the heavy rain and the enemy was defeated.

Deborah took no credit for the great victory because she knew her power came from God. Our strength and power today still come from God when we honor Him.

For Discussion

1. What was Deborah's job?

2. Why did the men of Israel lack leadership?

3. How did Deborah win a victory?

Speaking Puppet

What You Need

- puppet face pattern from page 24
- thin poster board
- crayons or markers
- spring-type clothespins
- scissors
- glue

Before Class

Duplicate the puppet face pattern for each child.

What to Do

1. Have the children color the puppet face using crayons or markers. Instruct them to make the lips and the lower mouth portion the same color (red or pink).

2. Instruct the students to glue the sheet to a piece of thin poster board.

3. Have the children cut out the puppet face along the outer solid lines. They should also cut a slit along the inner hair line up to the top dashed line.

4. Instruct the students to write the memory verse on the upper back of head.

5. Show how to fold the dashed lines to make the mouth movable.

6. Demonstrate how to glue a clothespin to the back mouth fold so that the mouth can be operated from behind the puppet.

Make It • Take It • Make It • Take It • Make It • Take It • Make It • Take It

24

Elisha

Ages 8-11

Memory Verse

I urge you to live a life worthy of the calling you have received.

~Ephesians 4:1

Worthy Elisha

Elisha was plowing in a field with oxen one day when Elijah came to him and threw his "mantle," or cloak, around him. This was a sign to Elisha that he was to succeed the prophet Elijah. Elisha quickly left his plowing and set out to follow Elijah and be his attendant. God knew Elisha would be a worthy prophet and would be of great value to Him.

When the Lord took Elijah to heaven in a chariot of fire, his spirit fell upon Elisha, who became a great prophet himself. Elisha saw many miraculous things as he walked the earth. He cured a Syrian commander of leprosy, he saw a widow's supply of oil replenished and he brought a Shunammite woman's son back to life. He performed the task of anointing kings-to-be in Syria and Israel.

Even though many times it was dangerous for him, Elisha always delivered the messages that God gave him. Throughout his life Elisha proved again and again that he was worthy of the trust God put in him. We should also prove worthy to God by following His Word and living the best Christian lives we can.

For Discussion

1. Why did Elijah throw his cloak around Elisha?

2. Name some miracles Elisha saw God perform.

3. Why was Elisha a worthy servant?

Make It • Take It • Make It • Take It • Make It • Take It • Make It • Take It

Straw Woven Mantle

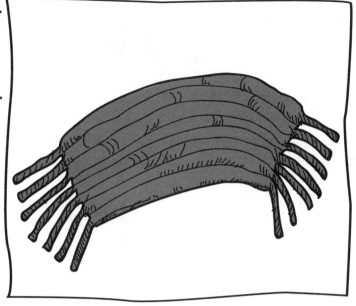

What You Need

- plastic drinking straws
- yarn balls
- tape
- twist ties
- scissors

Before Class

Cut six strands of yarn about 12" long per child. You will need one ball of yarn and three straws for each child.

What to Do

1. Have the students cut three straws in half.
2. Show how to thread one end of each yarn strand down inside each of the six straws.
3. Give each child a twist tie to join together the six strands of yarn at the bottom.
4. Have the students tape the top tip of each yarn strand securely to the straw through which it is threaded.
5. Show how to place a strip of tape across all six straws toward the bottom to hold them in place. (This is only to make handling the straws easier as you begin weaving. You will need to remove the tape after you do several rows because it will interfere with sliding down the yarn.)
6. Help the students as they leave a 3" length of yarn on one side and begin to work the yarn over and under the straws. They should continue over and under until they reach the last straw, then turn the work over and weave back the other way.
7. Show how to slide the weaved rows down the straws as you work. The children should keep sliding down the rows until they slide over the yarn tied at the bottom.
8. Allow the students to continue to make rows until they have the length of mantle they want.
9. To finish, show how to untie the twist tie at the bottom and tie the strands of yarn together in sets of two. This will hold the weaving tight as well as make fringe.
10. Help the students as they untape each strand at the top, slide the straw away from the yarn and tie these strands together in sets of two also. Tie the extra "tail" into one of the sets.

Esther

Memory Verse

Esther won the favor of everyone who saw her.

~Esther 2:15

Devoted Esther

There are only two books in the Bible that are named for women. One is Esther (the other is Ruth). Esther began her life as an orphan Jewish girl raised by her cousin Mordecai. The king, who did not know Esther was Jewish, chose her to be his queen because of her great beauty. God had a purpose for her in the palace.

A wicked man named Haman hated Jewish people so he demanded that the people bow down to him. Esther was opposed to Haman. She decided to go to her husband, the king, for her people. She knew that if the king became angry with her he could have her killed, but she stood ready to defend her people even if it meant losing her own life.

The wicked Haman planned to hang Esther's cousin Mordecai for not bowing to him but Esther found favor with the king. Because of her plea and God's intervention, the king ordered that Haman be hung instead. Beautiful Queen Esther won not only the hearts of her own people but the king's heart as well. He gave her the right to make laws to grant freedom to the Jews.

God used a small Jewish girl with a strong devotion to her people to carry out His plan. She became one of the Bible's greatest heroines because she served with intelligence, fearlessness and devotion.

For Discussion

1. Why did the king choose Esther for his queen?

2. Who did Esther defend?

3. What were the results of Esther's plea to the king?

A Crown of Jewels

What You Need

- crown pattern from page 29
- construction paper
- glue
- tape
- scissors
- stapler
- sequins, beads, glitter

Before Class

Duplicate the crown pattern for each child. Cut construction paper into 2 1/2" x 8" strips, two per child. You can provide any assortment of shiny, jewel-like materials for the students to decorate their crowns. Old costume jewelry can be cut apart to make beautiful "jewels." Even glitter and sequins combine well to give a rich feel to the crowns.

What to Do

1. Have the students cut out the crown pattern, trace it on brightly colored construction paper and cut it out.

2. Show how to tape a pre-cut strip to each side of the crown front.

3. Have the students write the memory verse on one of the strips, close to the taped area.

4. Allow the children to decorate the crown front with sequins, pearls, stars, etc.

5. Measure the crown to the child's head. Then hold the strips in place as you remove the crown from his or her head and staple the strips together.

6. Have the children cover the staples with tape to avoid injury.

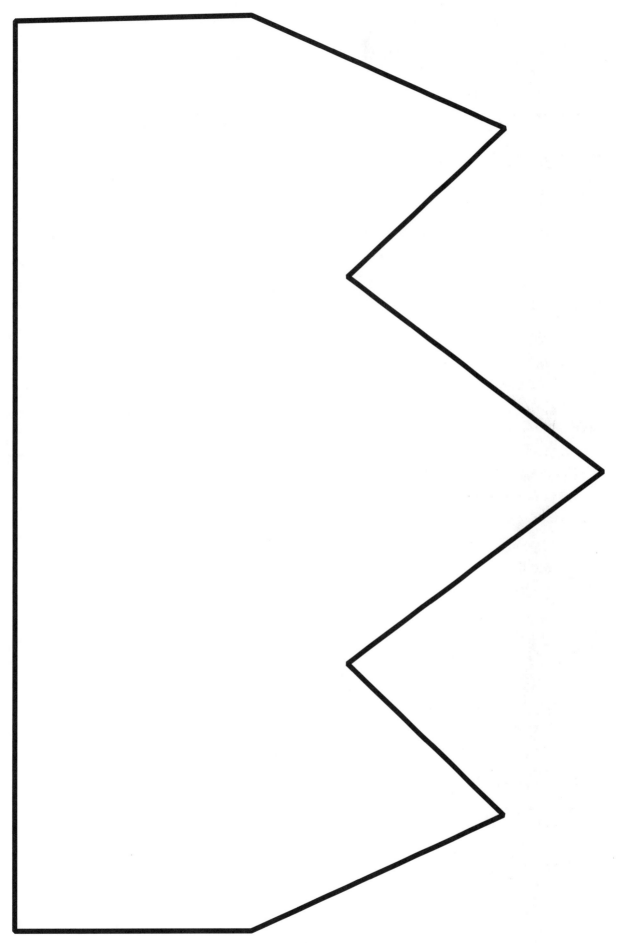

Gideon

Ages 8-11

Memory Verse

Have I not commanded you? Be strong and courageous.

~Joshua 1:9

Brave Gideon

The Midianites had taken the Israelites' land and crops, so God told Gideon He would help him rescue the Israelites. Gideon was skeptical. He asked God for a sign that this was really a message from Him, so God sent fire out of a rock. Gideon was then ready to lead the Israelites against the Midianites.

But then God said, "Wait. You have so many men that they will think they did it by their own strength instead of by My power. I will have to cut down the size of your army." Gideon started out with 32,000 soldiers but when God finished testing them, he had only 300 left to fight the mighty army of Midian.

Gideon was not by nature a very brave man, but as he learned to trust God his confidence grew. God told Gideon to make a surprise attack on the Midianites' camp at night using glowing torches while blowing trumpets and smashing pitchers. Gideon's men caused the Midianites to kill each other in the confusion. His men won a victory for the Israelites! The Israelites wanted to make Gideon king over them for his bravery but he said, "No, the Lord shall rule over you."

For Discussion

1. Who were Gideon's enemies?

2. How did Gideon know God was leading him?

3. How did the Israelites defeat the Midianites?

Make It • **Take It** • **Make It** • **Take It** • **Make It** • **Take It** • **Make It** • **Take It**

Rip Roaring Ring Toss

What You Need

- frozen whipped topping lids
- blue and green permanent markers
- heavy cardboard 12" x 12"
- construction paper
- paper towel tubes
- glue

Before Class

You will need four frozen whipped topping lids per child. Cut out the centers, leaving a $1/2$" ring. Cut the cardboard into 12" x 12" squares, one per child.

What to Do

1. Have the students color two of the rings blue and two green using permanent markers.

2. Instruct the children to cover a cardboard base with construction paper and glue it securely.

3. Have the students cover a paper towel tube with the same color of construction paper as used on the base, then glue it securely.

4. Show how to cut four slits in one end of the paper tube from the bottom up about 2".

5. Instruct the children to fold the slits up to make four tabs. They should place the tube in the center of the base and glue or tape the four tabs securely to the base.

6. Have the students write the memory verse on one corner of the base.

<u>**To Play the Game:**</u>

Each player takes two rings. Players take turns tossing their rings at the goal.

10 points are scored if they get the ring over the post.

5 points are scored if their ring is completely on the base but not over the post.

2 points are scored if any part of their ring is touching the base.

Play until an agreed upon total score is reached.

(Tossing distance should be determined by the age of the players.)

Hannah

Memory Verse

Hannah wept much and prayed to the Lord.

~1 Samuel 1:10

• •

Persistent Hannah

Have you ever wanted something so badly that you just kept asking for it and asking for it until you finally got it? Then what did you do? Did you show appreciation and gratitude to the person who gave it to you?

There is a story in the Bible about a lady named Hannah who did exactly that! She wanted a baby. She wanted one so much that she prayed every day for one. She prayed at home, she prayed at the temple — she prayed constantly that God would give her a child. She prayed for years!

Finally, God granted her desire and gave her a baby son. She named him Samuel, which means "asked of the Lord." But Hannah did not forget to show her thanks and gratitude to God for answering her prayer. When Samuel was old enough, she took him to the temple and left him there with Eli the priest so that he could serve God. It was not easy for Hannah to leave her small son, but she knew he was a gift from God. Returning him to God's service was her way of showing thanks.

If there is something special for which you are praying, don't give up. Be persistent like Hannah, but also remember to show appreciation when your prayers are answered. And remember that God does not always answer our prayers the way we want, but He does answer them in a way that He knows is best for us.

For Discussion

1. What does "persistent" mean?

2. For what was Hannah longing?

3. How did she show her appreciation for her answered prayer?

Zig Zag Place Mat

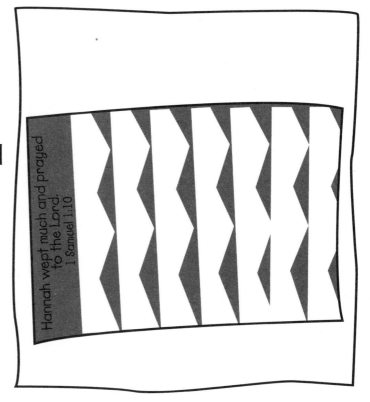

What You Need

- zig zag pattern from page 34
- construction paper
- scissors
- glue
- clear, self-stick plastic
- markers

Before Class

Duplicate the zig zag pattern for each child. Cut 13 1"x12" construction paper strips per child.

What to Do

1. Have the students fold an 18"x12" sheet of construction paper in half, bringing one short side over to meet the other short side.

2. Have the children cut out the zig zag pattern. Show how to hold the folded paper with the fold on the left, place the pattern on the fold horizontally and then trace the zig zag edge of the pattern five times in even rows from the bottom of the folded paper to the top.

3. Help the students cut the five lines, cutting through the fold, then unfold the sheet and lay it flat.

4. Show how to weave the pre-cut strips through the zig zag cuts, keeping them tightly together. Each one should be started from opposite ends of the weave.

5. Allow the students to glue down the tabs from the strips at the top and bottom of the larger sheet. Both sides should be glued.

6. Write or have the students write the memory verse on a plain edge of the weaved mat.

7. Cover the front and back of each place mat with clear, self-stick plastic.

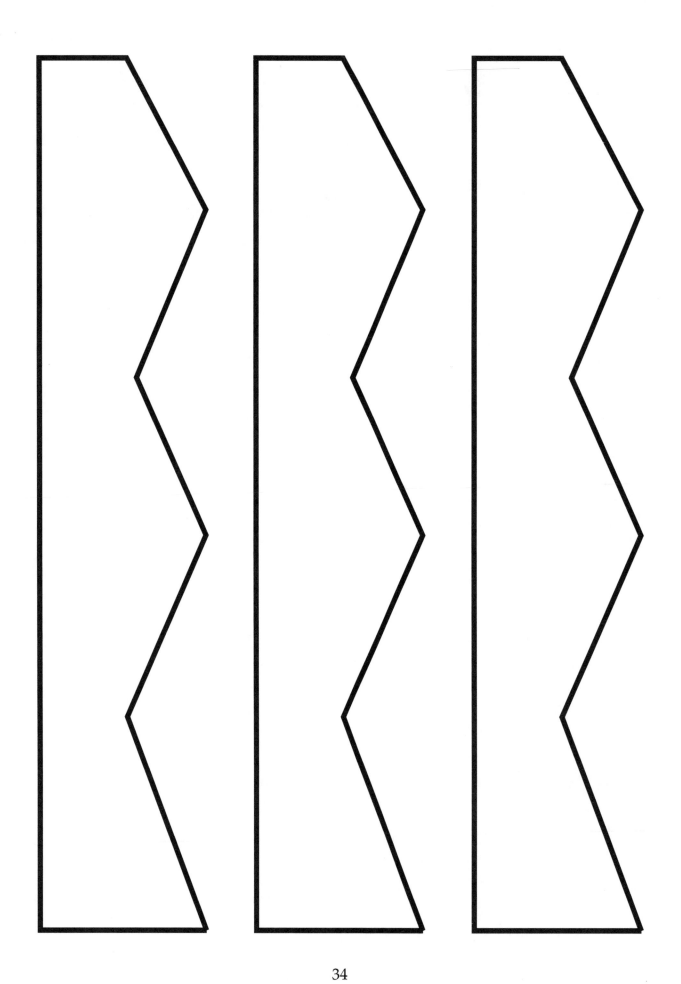

Isaac

Ages 5-8

Memory Verse

Trust in the Lord with all your heart.

~Proverbs 3:5

Trusting Isaac

Isaac was Abraham's son. Isaac had to learn trust at a very early age. When God tested his father's faith, Isaac went willingly to the mountain top where he was prepared to be a sacrifice. But God stopped Abraham and provided a ram instead. Isaac trusted his father to do God's will. Isaac was obedient.

When Isaac was old enough to get married, he trusted his father to choose a wife for him. When Abraham's servant brought back beautiful Rebekah for his bride, Isaac was thrilled.

Isaac and Rebekah spent many years together serving God. They were blessed with twin boys named Esau and Jacob. Esau was Isaac's favorite and Jacob was Rebekah's favorite. In his old age, Isaac's trusting nature was tried when he was tricked into giving his blessing and inheritance to his younger son, Jacob, instead of Esau.

To trust someone means to have confidence or faith in a person. As Isaac learned, when you trust God or people who are doing God's will, things will turn out right. But trusting people can also bring disappointment. Put your trust in God first.

For Discussion

1. How did Isaac trust his father?

2. How was Isaac's trust deceived by his son Jacob?

3. Why should we trust God instead of people?

Make It • Take It • Make It • Take It • Make It • Take It • Make It • Take It

Butterfly Beauty Magnet

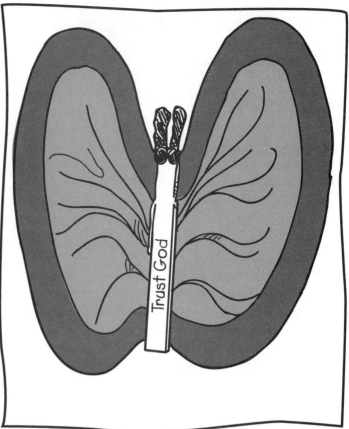

What You Need

- blue and yellow tissue paper
- wooden clothespins (not spring-type)
- hole punch
- safety scissors
- black construction paper scraps
- magnets
- markers
- black chenille stems

Before Class

Cut two blue sheets of tissue paper per child into 9" x 10" and two yellow sheets of tissue paper per child into 7" x 8".

What to Do

1. Show how to use safety scissors to round the corners of the blue and yellow tissue paper.

2. Have the students stack the yellow paper on the blue then fold it down the middle and unfold it.

3. Starting at the top center, demonstrate how to crunch the four layers together, holding them at the top and the bottom. Spread out the sheets at the sides for the butterfly's wings.

4. Help the students smear glue on the inside legs of a wooden clothespin. Push the layers of tissue up inside.

5. Allow the students to make two black eyes with a hole punch and a scrap of black construction paper. They should glue these to the front of the rounded head of the clothespin, then draw on a mouth with a marker.

6. Have the students cut a 3" piece of black chenille wire and bend it in half, then glue it to the back of the head for antennae.

7. Instruct the children to glue a large magnet on the back of the wooden clothespin.

8. Have the students write TRUST GOD on the front length of the butterfly's body.

Jacob and Esau

Ages 8-11

Memory Verse

He who conceals his sins does not prosper.

~Proverbs 28:13

The Twins and Deceit

The Bible tells about a set of twins named Jacob and Esau. Esau was the oldest. He was a hunter who loved the outdoors. Jacob was the younger twin. He stayed close to home. He was his mother's favorite.

In Bible times, the oldest son received the inheritance or blessing from his father. As the twins' father, Isaac, grew old and was almost blind, the twins knew he would pass on his blessing to Esau, the oldest. But Jacob's mother wanted him to receive the blessing instead of his brother, so she and Jacob made a plan to trick Isaac. Since he couldn't see well, she put goat skin on Jacob's arms so that Isaac would think that he was touching Esau's hairy arms and give Jacob the blessing.

The plan worked, but when Esau returned from hunting and found out what they had done, he was very angry. He wanted to kill Jacob, so Jacob had to escape to another country and live in exile for many years away from his family. Later in Jacob's life his own sons deceived him.

It doesn't pay to be deceitful. In the end, you are the one who ends up miserable. God is not pleased with deceit.

For Discussion

1. What did Esau like to do?

2. How did Jacob trick his father?

3. How did Jacob pay for his deceit?

Scratchy Paper Plate Puppet

What You Need

- face patterns from page 39
- 9" foam plates
- paper towel tubes
- construction paper
- coffee grounds
- black chenille wire
- yarn
- scissors
- craft glue

Before Class

Duplicate the face patterns for each child.

What to Do

1. Have the students write the memory verse on the inside of a foam plate.
2. Cut the eyes, nose and mouth pieces from construction paper using the patterns provided.
3. Show where to glue the face pieces on the back side of the plate.
4. Allow the students to cut several strands of yarn approximately 12" and glue them to the top rim of the plate for hair.
5. Have the students cut in half a 3" piece of chenille wire and glue on the pieces for eye brows.
6. Show how to smear the cheeks, chin and underneath the nose with glue, then liberally sprinkle the glue with coffee grounds to make a beard and mustache. Pour the excess back into the coffee can.
7. Instruct the students to cover a paper towel tube with construction paper and tape or glue it to hold.
8. Have the students cut two notches on opposite sides of one end of the tube.
9. Show how to slide the bottom rim of the plate into the notches and glue it in place.

Jehosheba

Ages 8-11

Memory Verse

The righteous are as bold as a lion.

~Proverbs 28:1

....

Jehosheba the Bold

Athaliah was a wicked woman whose son Ahaziah was king. When her son died, she had all of his sons killed so that they could not become king and rule over Judah. She wanted to rule!

What Athaliah didn't know was that King Ahaziah's half sister Jehosheba had stolen the king's infant son and hidden him. Jehosheba took the child to the temple where her husband was a priest. There they carefully hid her nephew Joash for six years. Jehosheba was very courageous to go against the wishes of Athaliah because she could have been killed. But she trusted God to take care of her and little Joash.

When Joash was nearly seven years old they revealed him as the rightful heir to the throne of Judah. Athaliah was angry, but the people rejoiced to have a righteous king again. The officers of the army put the wicked Athaliah to death.

Joash was only seven years old when he was crowned King of Judah. He reigned for 40 years. The Bible says he did what was right in the eyes of the Lord. It was all possible because his Aunt Jehosheba was bold enough to do what she knew was right. God gave her the courage to be bold. God will help us to be bold, too.

For Discussion

1. Why did Athaliah have all her grandsons killed?

2. What did Jehosheba do with the king's infant son?

3. How old was Joash when he became king?

Make It • Take It • Make It • Take It • Make It • Take It • Make It • Take It

Cool Tambourine

What You Need

- frozen whipped topping lids
- construction paper
- markers
- glue
- hole punch
- stickers
- jingle bells
- yarn

Before Class

You will need six jingle bells per child.

What to Do

1. Have the students trace and cut a circle of construction paper the same size as the inside of a the whipped topping lid.

2. Allow the students to write the memory verse on the circle and decorate it with stickers or draw musical notes on it.

3. Instruct the students to glue the circle to the top of the lid.

4. Help the children punch six sets of two holes each around the outside ring of the lid.

5. Have the students cut the yarn into six approximately 6" lengths.

6. Show how to string a jingle bell on each piece of yarn. They may want to tape the ends of the yarn for easier threading.

7. Show how to thread one end of the yarn through a hole in the lid, then put the other end through the next hole and tie securely. They should continue tying one jingle bell in each set of holes, then trim the ends of the yarn.

Jochebed

Ages 8-11

Memory Verse

Without faith it is impossible to please God.

~Hebrews 11:6

....

Faithful Jochebed

Jochebed was a mother who learned to trust God and to not doubt. She had strong faith in things she could not see. She depended on God's promises. She raised her children to love God and obey Him.

Jochebed's son Aaron was chosen to be a priest. He became the founder of the Hebrew priesthood. Jochebed's daughter Miriam led the Israelites in great faith as they crossed the Sea of Reeds.

But Jochebed's most well-known child was Moses, who grew to be a great leader. Jochebed was willing to give up her son so that he could fulfill God's plan. She trusted God to protect him as she set his baby basket floating down the Nile River. She did not know what Moses' future held, but God did and He allowed Jochebed to be a part of Moses' life for his first seven years, even though he was adopted by the pharaoh's daughter.

Jochebed's influence on her children's lives came from her great faith in the unseen. She believed in God, and that was enough for her.

For Discussion

1. Who were Jochebed's children?

2. How did she fulfill God's plan?

3. Describe what "faith" is.

Make It • **Take It** • **Make It** • **Take It** • **Make It** • **Take It** • **Make It** • **Take It**

Tin Can Pin Cushion

What You Need

- circle patterns from page 44
- foam rubber
- empty tuna cans
- felt
- table knives
- scissors
- craft glue
- construction paper
- stickers
- markers

Without faith it is impossible to please God. Hebrews 11:6

Before Class

Duplicate the circle patterns for each child.

What to Do

1. Have the students use the patterns to cut one small circle from foam rubber and one larger circle from felt.

2. Show how to spread a generous amount of glue inside a clean, empty tuna can.

3. Have the children lay the felt circle on the foam circle and place them inside the can.

4. Help the children use a table knife to tuck the edges of the felt down around the foam.

5. Have each students cut a strip of construction paper that is $1^1/_2$" x 11".

6. They should write the memory verse in the middle of the strip, then glue it around the outside of the can.

7. Allow the students to decorate the strip with stickers.

Make It • Take It • Make It • Take It • Make It • Take It • Make It • Take It

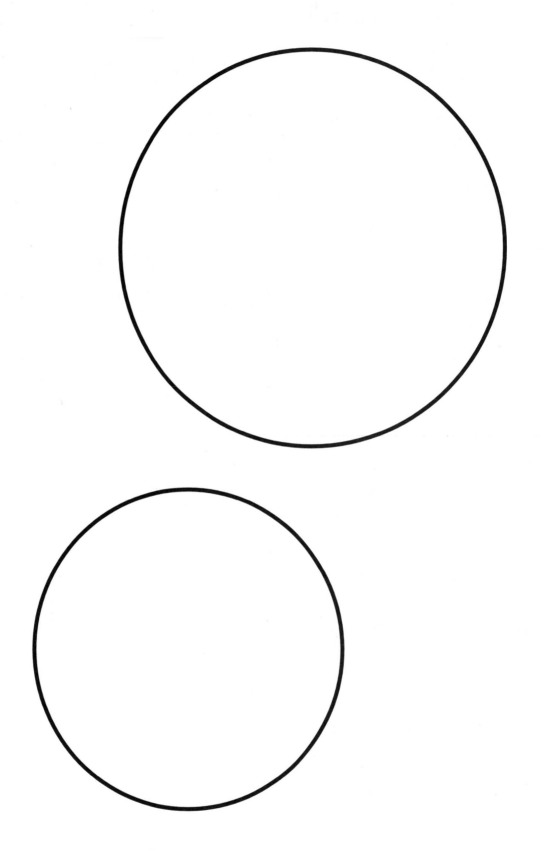

Jonah

Ages 5-8

Memory Verse

Will you not learn a lesson and obey my words?

~Jeremiah 35:13

Obedient Jonah

Jonah was a prophet. Prophets tell what will happen in the future. They are not like the "psychics" we hear about today because their messages did not come from their own ideas. They only gave messages that God told them to deliver.

God told Jonah to go to a city called Nineveh. He was to tell the people that they were sinning and must repent or else God would destroy their city. Nineveh was a very wicked city. Jonah didn't want to go there, so he hopped on a boat that was going the other way.

God does not like disobedience. He caused a great storm to rock the boat. Jonah knew that God caused the storm because of his disobedience, so he told the men to throw him overboard. As soon as they did, the storm stopped. But Jonah didn't drown; instead God sent a whale to swallow him. For three days and nights he stayed inside the smelly belly of the whale. He had lots of time to pray and ask God to forgive him for his disobedience. When the whale finally spat out Jonah on the shore, Jonah cleaned himself up and headed for Nineveh.

Sometimes we think it is hard to obey. We want to do things our own way. But disobedience will cause us trouble, just as it did for Jonah.

For Discussion

1. What is a prophet?

2. What did God tell Jonah to do?

3. How did he pay for his disobedience?

Wailer in a Whale

What You Need

- Jonah and memory verse patterns from page 47
- black construction paper
- scissors
- stapler
- crayons
- glue
- hole punch
- yarn
- thin poster board

Will you not learn a lesson and obey my words?
Jeremiah 35:13

Before Class

Duplicate the Jonah figure and memory verse from page 47 for each child. Cut the black construction paper into two 12" x 2" strips per child.

What to Do

1. Show how to lay the two construction paper strips on top of each other and staple at one end.

2. Help the students measure in about 3" and staple the other end. Show how to use a pencil to curl the ends — one up and one down.

3. Have the children color and glue Jonah to light poster board, then cut him out.

4. Show how to fold the tab back and staple Jonah inside the whale.

5. Assist the students in punching two holes in the top strip and putting a piece of yarn through them. Tie at the top.

6. Have the students cut out the memory verse and glue it to the top of the whale.

Will you not learn a lesson
and obey my words?

Jeremiah 35:13

Jonathan

Ages 5-8

Memory Verse

But there is a friend who sticks closer than a brother.

~Proverbs 18:24

Loyal Jonathan

Do you have a best friend? Is he or she almost as close to you as a brother or sister? David had a best friend. His name was Jonathan. Jonathan was a prince because his father was the king.

Jonathan and his friend David liked to spend time together laughing, talking, hunting or just sharing secrets. Jonathan's father, the king, became very jealous of David. He tried to have David killed several times. Jonathan, who was loyal to his friend David, warned David whenever his father flew into one of his rages. Sometimes he would help David escape to the safety of a cave or other hiding place until the king calmed down. Jonathan loved his friend and didn't want to see him hurt, even though it meant choosing loyalty to David over his father.

When Jonathan was killed in battle, David was deeply saddened. He knew he would not find another friend as loyal as Jonathan. You may have someone you love who is a loyal friend, but the Bible tells us that Jesus stays closer to us than a brother. That is loyalty!

For Discussion

1. What did David and Jonathan like to do together?

2. How did Jonathan show loyalty to his friend?

3. What are some good qualities in a friend?

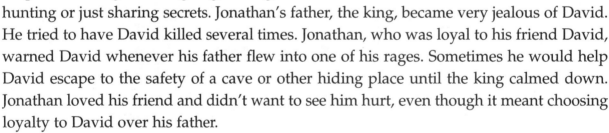

Make It • Take It • Make It • Take It • Make It • Take It • Make It • Take It

Cut Out Friends

What You Need

- pattern from page 50
- construction or poster paper
- scissors
- crayons
- marker

Before Class

Duplicate the pattern from page 50 for each child. You can tape together two 9" x 12" sheets of construction paper or use an 18" x 12" sheet of construction paper or white poster paper for this craft.

What to Do

1. Show how to accordion-fold the paper at approximately 3¼" intervals.

2. Have the students cut out and trace the pattern on the outside folded piece, placing the flat side on the fold and the mittened hand on the other side.

3. Instruct the students to carefully cut through all the layers, making sure they don't cut the folds.

4. Demonstrate how to gently pull apart and decorate the friends with crayons or markers.

5. Write or have the students write the memory verse on the back of the friends.

Make It • Take It • Make It • Take It • Make It • Take It • Make It • Take It

Joshua

Ages 8-11

Memory Verse

Be strong and courageous, because you will lead these people.

~Joshua 1:6

Bold Joshua

After Moses led the Israelites for 40 years from the Red Sea to the Jordan River, it was Joshua who led the second generation across the Jordan. He conquered kings, people and cities. He divided the Promised Land between the 12 tribes.

When Moses died, it was Joshua to whom God gave the boldness to take possession of the land. One such place was Jericho, a city surrounded by high, thick walls. For six days, Joshua had the Israelites parade around the city once a day with trumpets made of rams' horns. On the seventh day they circled the city seven times, blew the trumpets and shouted. The walls fell flat!

Joshua had great faith that God would help them conquer whomever they set out to conquer. After their victory at Jericho, the Israelites gained some of Joshua's boldness. It was with that courage and boldness that they continued to serve God throughout Joshua's lifetime. He was 110 years old when he died.

For Discussion

1. What great leader did Joshua follow?

2. Describe the fall of Jericho.

3. From where did Joshua's boldness come?

Make It • Take It • Make It • Take It • Make It • Take It • Make It • Take It

Potato Print Shield

What You Need

- shield pattern from page 53
- cardboard
- poster board
- tempera paint
- sharp knives
- scissors
- foam meat trays
- potatoes
- markers
- elastic
- wide tape
- glue

Be strong and courageous,
because you will lead these people.
Joshua 1:6

Before Class

Duplicate the shield pattern from page 53 for each child.

What to Do

1. Have the students cut out the shield pattern, then trace and cut one shield from poster board and one shield from cardboard.

2. Have them glue together the two shields.

3. Instruct the students to cut a small potato in half, crosswise. They should use a sharp knife (be sure to assist as needed) to cut away the four corners of the flat side to make a cross shape. They should cut approximately $1/2$" deep.

4. Have the students write the memory verse across the middle of the shield, then outline the shield with a complimentary color.

5. Instruct the students to cut two $4 1/2$" lengths of elastic and tape them to the back of the shield for holders.

6. Pour a small amount of paint into a meat tray. Show how to dab the potato stamp in the paint several times to remove excess, then print one cross on the bottom center of the shield and three in a row across the top.

52

Miriam

Ages 5-8

Memory Verse

A faithful man will be richly blessed.

~Proverbs 28:20

Trustworthy Miriam

In the first mention of Miriam in the Bible, she is 7 years old. A wicked ruler named Pharaoh had decreed that all Hebrew baby boys should be killed. Miriam's family was Hebrew. She had a baby brother named Moses whom she loved very much. She did not want him to be hurt.

Miriam's mother gave her an important job to do. She made a basket and put baby Moses in it. Miriam's mother instructed Miriam to watch the basket. Then she set the basket in the Nile River to float.

Carefully hiding in the reeds, Miriam watched until the basket floated to where Pharaoh's daughter, the princess, was bathing. The princess picked up the basket. Miriam knew that Moses would be safe because the princess would not let her father kill the baby she had found. Miriam came out of hiding and asked the princess if she would like her to find a nurse for the baby. When the princess agreed, Miriam went home and brought her mother to care for the baby. The princess did not know it was Moses' own mother! She took her to the palace. Moses' own mother got to raise her son after all.

God had a special plan for Moses, but it would not have been possible if Miriam had not been faithful in the job her mother gave her to do. She didn't question her mother, she just did what she was asked to do. God has jobs for all of us to do. All we need are listening ears and helping hands. Be faithful in what you are asked to do, whether it is big or small.

For Discussion

1. What job did Miriam's mother give her to do?

2. When the princess found Moses, what did she do?

3. How can we be faithful, even in small things?

54

Happy Helper Hands

What You Need

- hand pattern from page 56
- pink construction paper
- scissors
- paper fasteners
- ribbon
- markers

Before Class

Duplicate the hand pattern for each student.

What to Do

1. Have the children use the pattern to cut six hands from pink construction paper.

2. Instruct them to write one promise on each of five hands, such as "I will pick up my toys." One hand should say, "I will obey."

3. Have the students write "Helping Hands" on the sixth hand.

4. Show how to lay the hands in a stack with the "Helping Hands" hand on top. Assist in poking a paper fastener through the lower palm of the stack.

5. Have the students write the memory verse on the back of the last hand.

6. Help the children tie a 6" piece of ribbon into a bow and glue the bow to the front, covering the paper fastener.

Make It • Take It • Make It • Take It • Make It • Take It • Make It • Take It

Moses

Ages 5-8

Memory Verse

Now go, lead the people to the place I spoke of.

~Exodus 32:34

Moses the Leader

The awesome story of Moses began when he was just a small child. His mother put him in a basket and sent him down the river to save him from being killed. Pharaoh's daughter found him and raised him in the palace, but Moses never forgot that he belonged to the Hebrew people.

When Moses saw the Egyptians treating his people badly, he became angry. He killed an Egyptian taskmaster who was beating a Hebrew. Fearing for his life, he fled to Midian. There, God spoke to him from a burning bush. God told him that he must go back and free his people from Egypt and lead them to the Promised Land.

Pharaoh was not willing to let the Israelite people go. God had to send 10 plagues on the Egyptians before the Hebrew people were freed. Then Moses began the journey to lead the Hebrews to Canaan. But the task was not easy. The people were led into the desert and they often complained. Each time, Moses cried to the Lord and the Lord met their needs. God sweetened bitter water for them. He sent manna and quail when they were hungry.

God gave Moses a decree for His people. He said, "If you listen carefully to the voice of your Lord and do what is right in His eyes, and if you pay attention to His commands, I will not bring any harm on you like the Egyptians. I will take care of you." Moses was a good leader because he took his directions from God.

For Discussion

1. Who found and raised Moses?

2. How did God speak to Moses?

3. Why was Moses a good leader?

Sponge Painted Burning Bush

What You Need

- Moses pattern from page 59
- white poster board
- scissors
- glue
- markers
- sponges
- foam meat trays
- clothespins
- orange, red and yellow tempera paint

Now go, lead the people to the place I spoke of. Exodus 32:34

Before Class

Duplicate Moses from page 59 for each child. Cut white poster board into one 8" x 11" rectangle per child.

What to Do

1. Have the students color and cut out Moses.

2. Show where to glue Moses on the left side of the poster board.

3. Write or have the students write the memory verse across the top of the poster board.

4. Show how to use a black marker to sketch a bush's branches on the right side of the poster board.

5. Have the children cut a sponge into a ragged, round shape about the size of a half dollar, then pinch a spring-type clothespin in the center of the sponge.

6. Pour small amounts of red, yellow and orange paint into a meat tray.

7. Show how to dab the sponge into the colors, blending them.

8. Allow the students to repeatedly touch the sponge to the bush branches, dabbing them lightly all over.

Noah

Ages 8-11

Memory Verse

Noah was a righteous man, blameless among the people of his time.

~Genesis 6:9

Righteous Noah

Noah was a man God could trust. God looked down from heaven and saw that no one was living for Him, except Noah and his family. God decided it was time to destroy the wickedness and start over.

He gave Noah a big job to do: build an ark. God knew He could trust Noah to do it. People laughed and made fun of Noah when he built the ark and filled it with animals in a land where it never rained. But Noah obeyed God because he was righteous.

To be righteous means that you are worthy, just and without blame. God knew Noah was that kind of man because he lived his life to please God, not other people. He was rewarded for his righteousness by being spared from the Flood.

We should live our lives so that when God looks down at us, He will see a righteous person, just like He saw Noah.

For Discussion

1. Why were Noah and his family spared?

2. Why did Noah obey God?

3. How can we be righteous?

Make It • **Take It** • **Make It** • **Take It** • **Make It** • **Take It** • **Make It** • **Take It**

Noah's Critter Match Game

What You Need

- ark and animal patterns from pages 62 and 63
- thin white poster board
- markers or crayons
- construction paper
- scissors
- glue
- tape
- clear, self-stick plastic

Before Class

Copy one set of animal cards and the ark patterns for each child. Cut sheets of poster board into one $1/2$" x $1/2$" piece per child.

What to Do

1. Have the children evenly spread glue on a sheet of thin poster board then place a sheet of game cards on it. Allow the students to color or trace around the animals with markers.

2. Using the patterns, instruct the children to cut two of each piece from their choice of construction paper.

3. Show how to mount each of the two arks on a piece of poster board, then cut two more pieces the same size and put them behind the arks. Use tape to seal the three sides (not the top) to make a pocket.

4. Help the students cover the game card sheet with clear, self-stick plastic. Then have them cut apart the animal cards on the lines.

<u>Animal Match Game</u> (2 players)

The object of the game is to get the most animals in your ark. Shuffle all of the cards and lay them face down on the table. The first player should turn over two cards to see if they match. If they do, he or she should put them in his or her ark. If not, it is the next player's turn to do the same. Continue until all matches have been made. The player with the most animals in his or her ark wins!

61

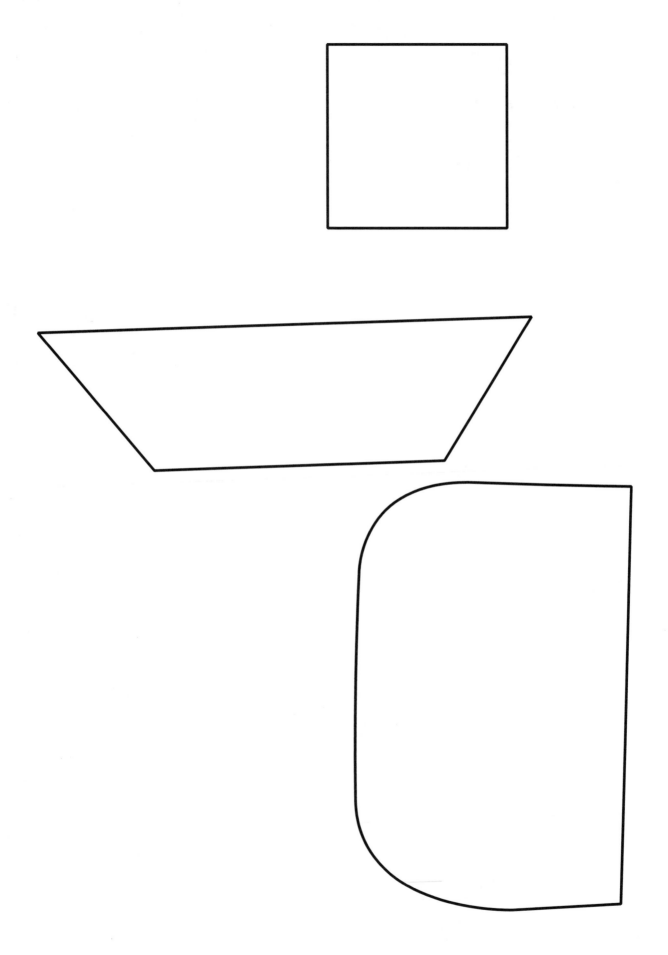

Pharaoh's Daughter

Ages 8-11

Memory Verse

The babe wept. And she had compassion on him.

~Exodus 2:6 KJV

....

The Compassionate Princess

The pharaoh — or ruler — of Egypt made a decree that all the Hebrew baby boys must be killed. One day as his daughter was taking her daily bath in the Nile River, the princess found a basket made of reeds. Inside the basket was a tiny baby boy. The princess had compassion for the baby and took him home to be raised in the palace.

Being Pharaoh's daughter meant that this young woman lived a life of luxury. She was pampered by many servants. She wore expensive clothes and she ate only the best fruit and meat. She could have been a very spoiled, self-centered girl, but we know she had a compassionate heart because she loved the little baby she found in the basket. Without knowing it, Pharaoh's daughter became part of God's divine will. She protected Moses, the future leader of the Israelites, from her father's harsh law.

The princess is not named in the Bible. She is referred to only as Pharaoh's daughter, a woman of compassion. But it was that gentleness of spirit that helped to save an entire Hebrew nation. When we are compassionate and loving toward others, we can also be part of God's plan for the world.

For Discussion

1. What did the princess find in the water?

2. What did she do about it?

3. What does it mean to have compassion?

Lovely Sun Catcher

What You Need

- patterns for heart and flowers from pages 66 and 67
- clear transparency sheets
- poster board
- hole punch
- permanent markers
- scissors
- string
- glue

Before Class

Duplicate the heart and flower patterns from pages 66 and 67 for each child. Cut the transparency sheets into one 7" x 8" piece per child.

What to Do

1. Show how to lay the flower pattern sheet underneath the transparency and trace the flowers onto the plastic with a black permanent marker.

2. Allow the children to color the flowers and leaves with permanent markers.

3. Have the students use the pattern to cut two heart frames from light weight colored poster board, using the pattern provided.

4. Show how to lay one frame flat, outline the inner edge with glue and lay the plastic on it. (Make sure the flowers are inside the cut "window.")

5. Have the students trim the plastic to fit inside the frame shape.

6. Instruct the students to glue the second frame on top.

7. Have the students write the memory verse on the clear plastic between the flowers using permanent marker.

8. Help the students punch a hole in the top center of the heart for hanging.

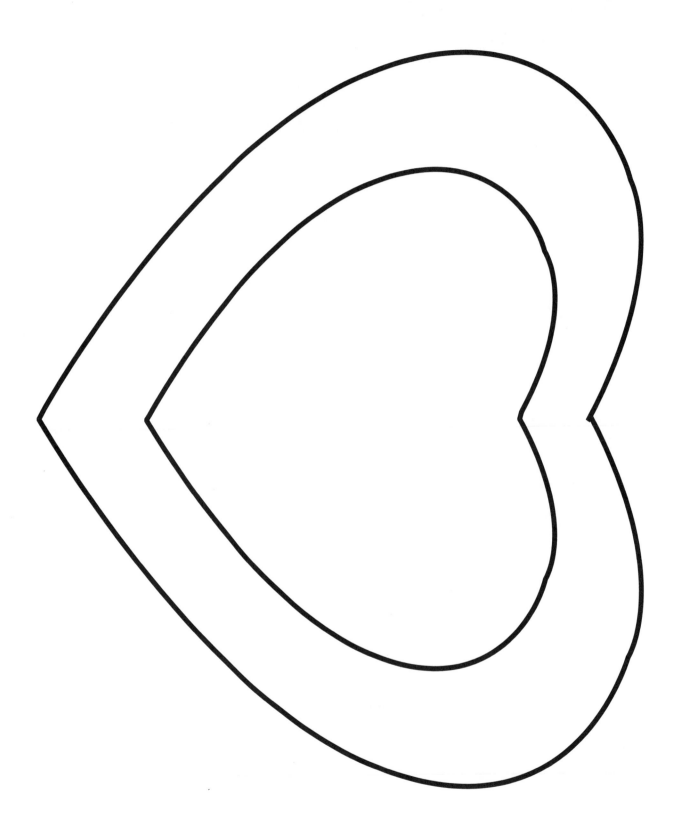

Rachel

Ages 5-8

Memory Verse

Know that the testing of your faith develops perseverence.

~James 1:3

Patient Rachel

Rachel was a beautiful maiden girl who cared for her father's sheep. Each day she brought the sheep to the watering hole for a drink of water. One day, a young man named Jacob saw her there and fell in love with her. Since he had no money, he asked her father if he could work for him as a shepherd for seven years to gain the right to marry Rachel. Her father agreed. The Bible says that the time passed quickly because he was so eager to have Rachel for his wife.

When the seven years were finally over and it was time for the marriage, Rachel's father decided that his older daughter, Leah, should get married first. He tricked Jacob into thinking he was marrying Rachel, but it was her sister Leah under the bridal veil.

In Bible times, men could have more than one wife, so Rachel waited patiently for another seven years while Jacob worked again for her father so he could marry her. After a total of 14 years, Jacob and Rachel were finally husband and wife. God blessed them with children, including one very special son named Joseph. It is not always easy to persevere, especially when you are waiting for something you really want. But God will reward you for working hard to accomplish His will.

For Discussion

1. What was Rachel's job?

2. Why did Rachel's father trick Jacob into marrying Leah?

3. How long did Rachel wait for Jacob?

Terrific Craft Stick Trivet

What You Need

- thin craft sticks
- craft glue
- permanent markers

Before Class

You will need 15 thin craft sticks per student.

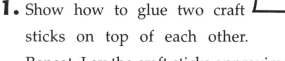

What to Do

1. Show how to glue two craft sticks on top of each other. Repeat. Lay the craft sticks approximately $4\frac{1}{2}$" apart.

2. Have the students pour a thick line of craft glue across the top of each set.

3. Demonstrate how to start laying sticks across, between the two doubled pieces, gluing one end to each of the base set of sticks (11 sticks should fit).

4. Allow a short drying time.

5. Have the students write the memory verse on the trivet with permanent markers, then decorate it any way they choose using permanent markers.

Rahab

Ages 5-8

Memory Verse

Be strong and courageous.

~Deuteronomy 31:6

Courageous Rahab

Joshua, the leader of Israel, sent two men from the Israelite army to secretly spy on Jericho. Joshua had plans to conquer the city. He needed this information to plan his best attack.

Rahab was a woman who lived in Jericho. In fact, her house was built over a gap between the two walls of Jericho. When the spies needed a place to hide in Jericho, they went to Rahab's house and asked for help. She hid them under a pile of flax on her roof top until night. Then she hoisted them down the outside wall of the city from her window using a basket and heavy rope.

Rahab told the spies she had faith in their God. When Joshua's army attacked the city, they told Rahab to mark her house with a scarlet rope outside her window so that they would know not to destroy her home. Rahab's courage was part of God's plan for Joshua to conquer the city of Jericho.

Sometimes we are asked to do things that are very difficult, but if we are courageous God will give us the strength we need to do them. Just ask Him!

For Discussion

1. Where was Rahab's house?

2. What happened when two spies came to her house?

3. How did Rahab's courage help fulfill God's plan?

Basket Over the Wall

What You Need

- basket pattern from page 72
- foam meat trays
- foam packing chips
- glue
- brown construction paper
- yarn
- markers
- scissors
- tape

Before Class

Cut a 5" x 1/2" opening in the top rim of the foam meat trays, one per child. Duplicate the basket pattern for each child. Cut yarn into 7" lengths, two per child.

What to Do

1. Have the students spread a thick layer of glue along the bottom rim of the meat tray and lay a row of packing chips all the way across, placing each one in an opposite direction of its neighbor. Repeat until the wall fills the tray.

2. Instruct the students to trace the basket pattern on brown construction paper and cut it out.

3. Show how to make slash marks on the front of the basket with a marker to look like weaves.

4. Show how to tape one end of the yarn to the back of the basket and one end to the middle back of the tray, through the hole. Repeat for the other side of the basket.

5. Write or have the students write the memory verse on the back of the tray.

6. Demonstrate how to push the basket through the opening from the back and let it down over the wall as you tell the story of Rahab.

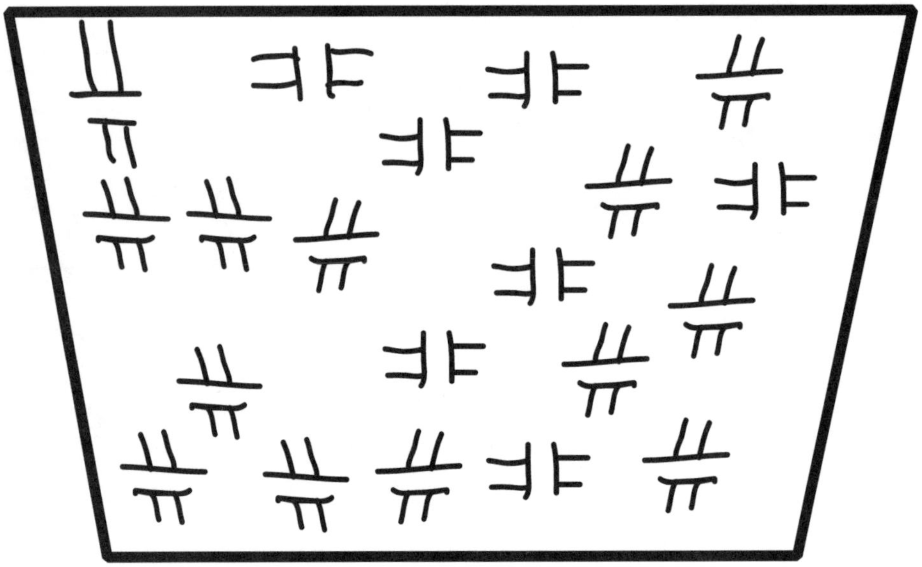

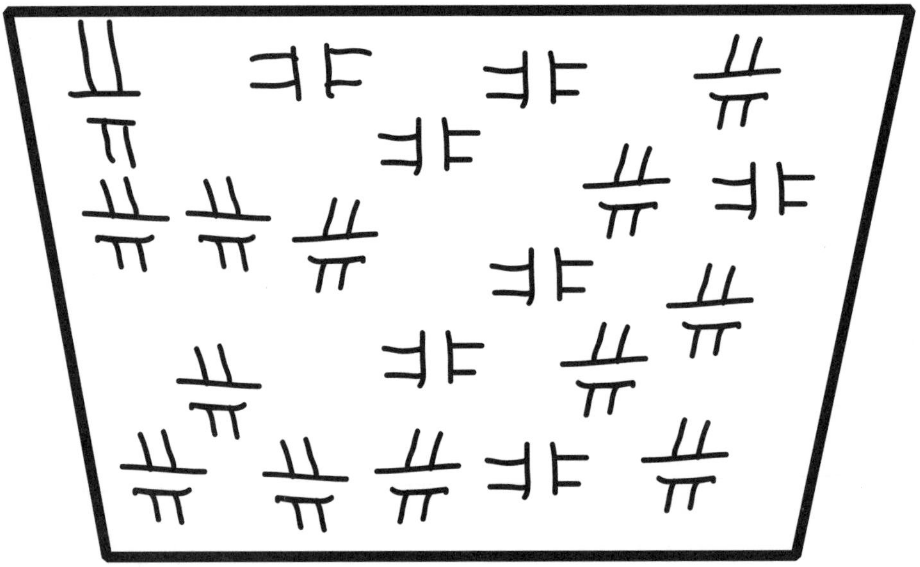

Rebekah

Ages 8-11

Memory Verse

Be kind and compassionate to one another.

~Ephesians 4:32

. . . .

Kind Rebecca

Rebekah was a young woman whose job was to go to the well to get water. She did not know that one evening a stranger from far away would see her there. He was in town to find a wife for Isaac, his master's son. God said that the servant would know he had found the right woman when she offered him and his camels a drink of water.

Rebekah offered water to the man to drink. Then she made several more trips to get water for his camels. She invited the stranger to go to her family's home for the night. She did not know the man's purpose for being there. She was simply offering kindness to a stranger. When she and the servant arrived at her father's house, the man explained that he wanted Rebekah to go with him to marry his master's son. Rebekah had no idea who she was marrying, but she felt that it was right, so she left her family and went with the man to a new land.

Rebekah helped to fulfill God's plan because she was willing to be a servant. She offered water to a stranger out of kindness and ended up marrying a man who was an heir to much wealth. Kindness was Rebekah's nature. God rewarded her. God rewards us for the kindness we show to others, too.

For Discussion

1. What was Rebekah's job?

2. How did her kindness to a stranger change her life?

3. How did Rebekah fulfill God's plan?

Kindness Baskets to Share

What You Need

- construction paper
- gift wrap
- foil gift wrap
- scissors
- spray adhesive
- stapler
- markers
- silk flowers

Before Class

Cut the construction paper, gift wrap and foil gift wrap into 9" x 9" sheets, one of each per child.

What to Do

1. Show how to glue gift wrap to one side of the construction paper and glue foil gift wrap to the other side of the construction paper. (You can use regular glue for this, but spray adhesive allows a smoother finished look.)

2. Demonstrate how to cut a $1^1/_2$" circle through all three layers in one corner.

3. Have the students place the square so the corner with the hole is at the top. Show how to fold the two sides toward the center.

4. Show how to pull up the bottom point and staple it to the two side pieces.

5. Have the students write the memory verse on a slip of paper and glue it to the lower back of the basket.

6. Allow the children to fill the "basket" with silk flowers. Encourage the students to give the Kindness Basket to a friend or family member who is need of kindness.

Ruth

Ages 8-11

Memory Verse

He who loves me will be loved by my Father.

~John 14:21

Loving Ruth

Do you like love stories? There is a very special love story in the Bible about a lady named Ruth. Ruth lived with her mother-in-law, Naomi, and her sister-in-law because their husbands had all died. When Naomi decided to go back to her homeland, Ruth went with her because she didn't want Naomi to be alone.

After they arrived in Bethlehem, Ruth had to pick up pieces of grain that fell by the edge of the fields when the fields were harvested. It was very hard work but she did not complain because the work helped to support her and her mother-in-law. One day, the man who owned the fields came by and saw the pretty young woman working there. His name was Boaz. He decided right then that he would always protect and take care of Ruth — like love at first sight! Ruth and Boaz were married.

Ruth's loving ways brought her to a foreign land, but God worked a miracle in Ruth's life. He provided someone to love and take care of her because she had shown love to those around her.

When we show love to others it spreads like rays of sunshine to everyone it touches. God rewards a loving person.

For Discussion

1. Why did Ruth choose to live with Naomi?

2. Where did Boaz find Ruth?

3. How did God reward Ruth's loving and gentle ways?

Love Mobile

What You Need

- heart patterns from pages 77 and 78
- plastic container lids
- poster board
- hole punch
- markers
- doily hearts
- lace
- glue
- scissors
- yarn
- yarn needles
- rulers

Before Class

Duplicate the heart patterns from pages 77 and 78 for each child.

He who loves me will be loved by my father. John 14:21

What to Do

1. Have the students glue a strip of lace around the outside edge of a plastic lid. They can use clothespins to hold the lace as it dries. Set aside.

2. Have the students cut out the patterns and trace them on poster board. They should cut and trace one large, two medium and two small hearts.

3. Allow the students to decorate the two medium and two small hearts any way they choose. They can use paper doilies for a quick and attractive way to decorate them.

4. Have the children write the memory verse on both sides of the large heart.

5. Show how to punch a hole near the top of each heart.

6. Have the students measure three 8" lengths of yarn, one 13" length of yarn and two 10" lengths of yarn.

7. Show how to thread an 8" piece of yarn into the yarn needle. Pull the piece of yarn up through the center of the plastic lid, leave a loop of yarn for hanging and go back down through the lid. Tie the ends together.

8. Have the children tie one end of the 13" piece of yarn to the large heart then tie the other end to the yarn underneath the lid center.

9. Show how to tie the other lengths of yarn to each of the small and medium hearts. The students should thread the other end of the yarn through the needle and pull it up through the rim of the lid. Help the children to remove the needle and tie the yarn in a knot.

Samson

Ages 5-8

Memory Verse

The Lord is my strength and my song.

~Exodus 15:2

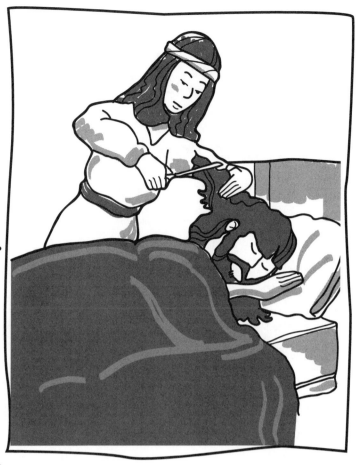

. . . .

Strong Samson

Do you know who was the strongest man who ever lived? It wasn't Arnold Swartzeneggar or Hulk Hogan, but a man in the Bible named Samson. Do you know why he was so strong? It was because God gave special instructions to his parents and said if they followed them, He would give great strength to their son Samson. One of God's instructions was that they were never to cut Samson's hair.

Samson's parents obeyed God's command and Samson grew to be a strong, handsome young man. At first, Samson used his strength wisely against his enemies, the Philistines. Then he fell in love with a Philistine girl named Delilah. The Philistine leaders paid her a lot of money to find out the secret of Samson's strength. At first, Samson just teased Delilah, but finally he gave in and told her that his hair was the key to his strength.

Knowing Samson's secret, the Philistines cut off Samson's hair while he slept and easily captured him. In prison, Samson asked God to forgive him and let him gain back his strength. God granted Samson's prayer, but Samson died along with the Philistines as he pulled down the pillars of the temple on thousands of his enemies.

God was the real source of Samson's strength. He is also the source of our strength against our enemy, Satan.

For Discussion

1. Why was Samson so strong?

2. How did Samson use his strength wisely?

3. What happened when Samson chose a "bad" friend?

Growing Hair Cups

What You Need

- face patterns from page 81
- plastic cups
- construction paper
- permanent markers
- potting soil
- glue
- scissors
- grass seed

Before Class

Duplicate the pattern page for each child.

What to Do

1. Have the students cut out the patterns, trace them on construction paper and cut them out. They may use any colors, although pink works well for the ears and nose, red for the mouth, white for the outer eye and black for the inner eye.

2. Write or have the students write the memory verse on the back of the cup with a permanent marker.

3. Show how to glue the face to the cup.

4. Help the students fill the cup $3/4$ full with potting soil.

5. Allow them to sprinkle a few grass seeds on top of the soil, then cover the seeds lightly with soil.

6. Assist the children as they water the plants and set Samson in a sunny window. As his "hair" begins to grow, they can "trim" it with scissors.

Samuel

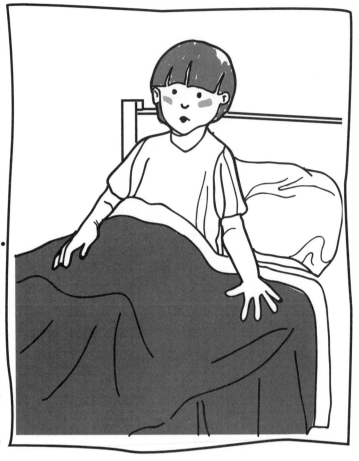

Ages 5-8

Memory Verse

Speak, Lord, for your servant is listening.

~1 Samuel 3:9

Submissive Samuel

Samuel grew up in the temple with Eli the priest. His mother had prayed a very long time for a child, so when God blessed her with Samuel, she promised to give him back to the Lord's service when he was old enough to leave home. Every year she came to the temple to see him and bring him a new coat.

One night when Samuel was in bed, he heard someone call his name. He quickly ran to Eli. But Eli hadn't called him so he sent Samuel back to bed. Again the voice called his name and Samuel ran to Eli. Now Eli realized it must be God's voice, so he told Samuel to answer and listen to what God told him. The next time Samuel heard his name called, the submissive Samuel told God he was listening. The message God gave him was not very pleasant, because it was about Eli the priest. God told Samuel that one day Samuel would replace Eli. Eli's house would be destroyed because his sons were sinful.

A submissive person is someone who totally obeys the Lord. Samuel continued to be submissive and obedient to God's voice throughout his life. He learned when he was young how important it was to listen and do what God asked of him.

For Discussion

1. Why did Samuel live at the temple?

2. How did God speak to Samuel?

3. Why is it important to be listening for God's voice?

Make It • Take It • Make It • Take It • Make It • Take It • Make It • Take It

Stylish Speak Banner

What You Need

- banner pattern and memory verse from page 84
- felt
- plastic drinking straws
- sequins
- yarn
- craft glue
- scissors
- small Bible pictures
- clothespins

Before Class

Duplicate the banner and memory verse patterns for each child. Cut the straws into 6¹/₂" pieces, one per child. Cut one 18" length of yarn per child. The Bible pictures can be cut from old greeting cards, magazines or stickers.

What to Do

1. Have the students cut out the banner pattern and trace it on any color of felt, then cut it out.

2. Show how to drop glue on the straw and wrap the top of the banner around it. Allow the students to use the clothespins to hold the banner in place for drying while you go on to the next step.

3. Show how to use craft glue to write SPEAK, one letter at a time, across the top of the banner. Have the children lay sequins in the glue as they finish each letter.

4. Have the students cut out and glue the memory verse beneath the sequined word.

5. Give each student a picture of a Bible to glue on the banner below the memory verse.

6. Show how to thread the pre-cut length of yarn through the straw, tying it at the top. Remove the clothespins.

Speak, Lord, for
your servant is listening.
1 Samuel 3:9

Sarah

Memory Verse

I will bless her...so that she will be the mother of nations.

~Genesis 17:16

Mother Sarah

Sarah was Abraham's wife. Back in Bible times, little importance was placed on a woman until she gave her husband a son. Sarah's early life was particularly tragic because she did not have any children. But she remained loyal to Abraham. She went wherever he went, even when he spent many years roaming from country to country. Sarah shared the dangers, the disappointments and the joys with her husband.

One day when Sarah and Abraham were very old, three visitors came to see them. Sarah made cakes for them on a stone fireplace as they delivered a message to Abraham. The men were angels sent by God to tell Abraham that Sarah would soon have a son. Sarah laughed at them because she thought she was too old to have a baby.

But God kept His word because Sarah had been faithful. So even though she was old, Sarah gave birth to a son. They named him "Isaac." Sarah was a tender, loving mother who raised her son with a gentle influence. Sarah's name lives on as the mother of nations because her faith helped to achieve one of the miracle births in the Bible.

For Discussion

1. To whom was Sarah married?

2. Who were the three visitors?

3. Why is Sarah called the "mother of nations"?

Make It • Take It • Make It • Take It • Make It • Take It • Make It • Take It

Bouncing Baby Booties

What You Need

- bootie patterns from page 87
- poster board
- markers
- scissors
- hole punch
- yarn
- ribbon
- stapler

I will bless her... so that she will be the mother of nations. Genesis 17:16

Before Class

Make cardboard templates of the two booties patterns from page 87. Cut two 15" lengths of white yarn per child. Cut one 10" length of pink ribbon per child.

What to Do

1. Have the children trace and cut two booties from blue poster board. (You can also use white and color them blue.)

2. Instruct the students to punch out the holes as indicated on the pattern.

3. Write or have the students write half of the memory verse on each bootie. Make sure that the booties are facing opposite directions when the verse is written, with the toes pointed out.

4. Show how to use yarn to lace each bootie and tie at the top.

5. Allow the students to outline the booties with a complimentary color of marker.

6. Help the children staple the booties together at the top inside edge.

7. Instruct the students to tie the ribbon in a bow and glue it at the top of the two booties where they are joined together.

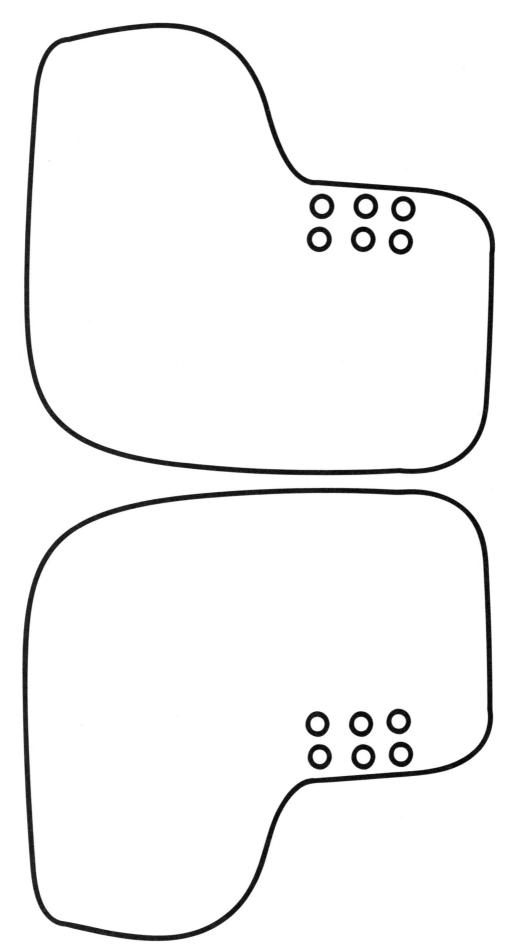

The Shunammite

Ages 8-11

Memory Verse

But thanks be to God! He gives us the victory.

~1 Corinthians 15:57

....

The Victorious Shunammite

Sometimes the Bible does not give a first or last name to people but instead identifies them by the land they lived in. This is the case of the Shunammite. She lived in the village of Shunem. But even though the Bible doesn't tell us her name, her story is of great importance.

The Shunammite was a wealthy and influential woman. Because she lived on the edge of a well traveled road, many people passed her home. One of them was the prophet Elisha. She had heard stories about this man of God. She convinced her husband to make a special room upstairs for Elisha so he could stay there whenever he visited the area. On one of his visits he told the woman, who did not have any children, that in the spring she would have a son. It came true, just as Elisha prophesied.

About 12 years later, the Shunammite's son became sick and died. She did not wail or cry but simply carried her son up to Elisha's bed and then went to find Elisha. Her faith was so great that she never once said, "My son is dead." Instead, when Elisha asked about her son she said, "It is well." When Elisha arrived at the room where the boy lay, he shut the door and prayed to God. Suddenly the boy sneezed and opened his eyes.

From beginning to end, the story of the Shunammite woman is an example of faithful living. She did not allow herself to have negative ideas. Instead, she put her trust in the power of God.

For Discussion

1. Why was this woman called a Shunammite?

2. What did she ask her husband to do for Elisha?

3. How did God reward the woman's kindness and faith?

Perky Plant Holder

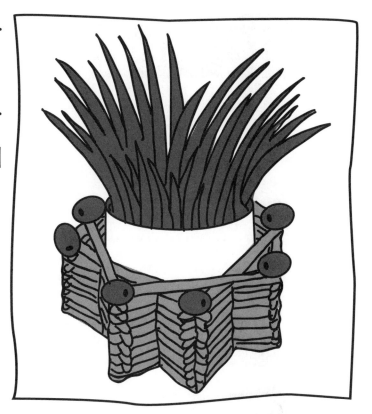

What You Need

- thin craft sticks
- craft glue
- wooden beads
- cardboard
- felt
- markers

Before Class

Cut cardboard into 5" x 5" squares, one per child. You will need 80 craft sticks and eight beads per child. If you have a young or less skilled class, glue down the first two layers of sticks before the children arrive. It will be easier for them to follow.

What to Do

1. Give each child a cardboard base and have them trace and cut a piece of felt and glue it to the cardboard.

2. Have the students flip the base over so the felt is on the bottom. Show how to glue four craft sticks in a square shape on top of the base.

3. Show how to glue four more craft sticks in a diagonal shape across the square. The students should continue the back and forth process until they have 20 layers.

4. Allow the students to glue a wooden bead to each of the eight points of the star.

5. Have the students write the memory verse on a piece of paper and glue it to the inside bottom of the plant holder.

Make It • Take It • Make It • Take It • Make It • Take It • Make It • Take It

Solomon

Ages 5-8

Memory Verse

God gave Solomon wisdom.

~1 Kings 4:29

Wise Old Solomon

Solomon was a king of Israel. Unlike some of the others who had been king, Solomon did not call for war on other nations. He preferred to work on gaining great wealth. Early in his reign, God spoke to him and asked him to name a gift he wanted. Solomon asked for wisdom. God was so pleased that He gave him not only wisdom, but riches and a long life as well.

Solomon displayed his wisdom when two women came to him with one baby, each claiming to be its mother. He solved the problem by ordering the child to be cut in two so each woman could have half. Solomon knew that the real mother would rather give her child to the other woman than see it hurt, so when one of the women begged him to stop, Solomon knew the baby belonged to her.

Solomon spent a great deal of time building the beautiful temple that his father, David, had planned. He also had men go to the far end of the Red Sea and bring back gold, timber and precious stones for the temple.

Solomon used his gifts of wisdom from God to serve Him. As long as he did, God blessed him. God will bless us if we use the gifts He has given wisely.

For Discussion

1. For what gift did Solomon ask?

2. How did he use his gift to serve God?

3. What gift has God given you?

Make It • Take It • Make It • Take It • Make It • Take It • Make It • Take It

String King

What You Need

- puppet patterns from page 92
- paper fasteners
- paper towel tubes
- felt
- glue
- scissors
- hole punch
- toilet tissue rolls
- yarn or string
- wiggle eyes
- markers
- tape

Before Class

Duplicate the puppet patterns from page 92 for each child.

What to Do

1. Have the students cover a toilet tissue roll with felt and glue it securely.
2. Instruct them to cut out the puppet patterns and trace them on felt, then cut those out.
3. Show how to use paper fasteners to attach the legs to the bottom front of the roll.
4. Show how to overlap the ends of the arms and lay them on the center top of the cape, then put a paper fastener through all three layers and attach the cape and arms to the top center of the back of the toilet tissue roll.
5. Have the students glue the crown to the top of the head and glue two wiggle eyes to the face. They can glue sequins on the crown. Show how to make a nose and mouth from felt scraps and glue those to the face. The head should be glued to the front center of the toilet tissue roll.
6. Use a hole punch to make a hole in each hand and one in the top center of the crown for each child.
7. Have the students cover a paper towel tube with construction paper and glue it securely.
8. Encourage the students to write the memory verse across the front of the tube.
9. Help the students attach string or yarn to the hands and crown, through the holes. Assist in tying the other ends of the string around the tube. Tape in place.

Widow of Zarephath

Ages 8-11

Memory Verse

My God will meet all your needs.

~Philippians 4:19

The Needy Widow

The widow of Zarephath was a woman whose husband had died. She and her son were alone and they were very poor. There was a drought in their homeland and there was a famine.

As the widow was about to make a little cake with the very last of her supplies, Elijah the prophet approached her house. He asked her to give him something to eat and drink. She told him that all she had was enough for one small cake and then she and her son would die because they had nothing more to eat.

But Elijah insisted that if she gave him something to eat first that she and her son would have plenty. She must have felt skeptical, but the widow did as she was told. As soon as she fried the cake for Elijah she returned to her barrel to find plenty of meal to make more food for her and her son. God continued to supply oil and meal for the widow of Zarephath throughout the drought.

The widow and her son never went hungry because she was willing to give all she had. She was also willing to believe and have faith. God will supply all our needs if we follow the example of the widow of Zarephath.

For Discussion

1. Describe the widow's condition before Elijah came.

2. Why did the widow obey Elijah's request?

3. How did God continue to meet her needs?

Bird Feeder Ornament

What You Need

- bird feeder patterns from page 95
- colored foam meat tray
- clear plastic communion cups
- bird seed
- poster board
- crayons
- yarn
- yarn needle
- scissors
- glue

Before Class

Duplicate the patterns for each child.

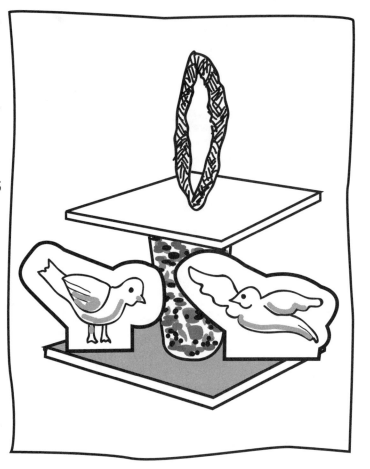

What to Do

1. Have the students use the patterns to cut two squares from the colored foam meat trays.

2. Show how to use a yarn needle to pull a piece of yarn through the center of the smaller square, then back down, tying on the underneath side while leaving a 2" loop on top for hanging.

3. Instruct the children to glue the bottom of a clear plastic communion cup or medicine cup to the center of the larger foam square.

4. Have the students color the birds, then glue them to thin poster board and cut them out.

5. Show how to fold back the tabs on the birds and glue them to each of two corners of the feeder bottom.

6. Help the students fill the plastic cup with bird seed.

7. Have the children drop a line of glue around the rim of the cup and set the smaller square on it.

8. Instruct the children to write the memory verse on a slip of paper and glue it to the bottom of the feeder. Allow to dry overnight.